Act Three, Scene Five

by Terry Ortwein

Single copies of plays are sold for reading purposes only. The copying or duplicating of a play, or any part of play, by hand or by any other process, is an infringement of the copyright. Such infringement will be vigorously prosecuted.

Baker's Plays
7611 Sunset Blvd.
Los Angeles, CA 90042
bakersplays.com

NOTICE

This book is offered for sale at the price quoted only on the understanding that, if any additional copies of the whole or any part are necessary for its production, such additional copies will be purchased. The attention of all purchasers is directed to the following: this work is fully protected under the copyright laws of the United States of America, the British Commonwealth, including Canada, and all other countries of the Copyright Union. Violations of the Copyright Law are punishable by fine or imprisonment, or both. The copying or duplication of this work or any part of this work, by hand or by any process, is an infringement of the copyright and will be vigorously prosecuted.

This play may not be produced by amateurs or professionals for public or private performance without first submitting application for performing rights. Licensing fees are due on all performances whether for charity or gain, or whether admission is charged or not. Since performance of this play without the payment of the licensing fee renders anybody participating liable to severe penalties imposed by the law, anybody acting in this play should be sure, before doing so, that the licensing fee has been paid. Professional rights, reading rights, radio broadcasting, television and all mechanical rights, etc. are strictly reserved. Application for performing rights should be made directly to BAKER'S PLAYS.

No one shall commit or authorize any act or omission by which the copyright of, or the right to copyright, this play may be impaired. No one shall make any changes in this play for the purpose of production.

Publication of this play does not imply availability for performance. Both amateurs and professionals considering a production are strongly advised in their own interest to apply to Baker's Plays for written permission before starting rehearsals, advertising, or booking a theatre.

Whenever the play is produced, the author's name must be carried in all publicity, advertising and programs. Also, the following notice must appear on all printed programs, "Produced by special arrangement with Baker's Plays."

Licensing fees for ACT THREE, SCENE FIVE are based on a per performance rate and payable one week in advance of the production.

Please consult the Baker's Plays website at www.bakersplays.com or our current print catalogue for up to date licensing fee information.

Copyright © 1986, 1987 by Terry Ortwein
Made in U.S.A.
All rights reserved.

ACT THREE, SCENE FIVE
ISBN **978-0-87440-081-6**
#101-B

ACT THREE, SCENE FIVE was first produced at Choate Rosemary Hall, Wallingford, Connecticut, in November, 1986. This production was directed by the playwright, and the cast was as follows:

CHRIS	Tom Deck
PATTY	Laura Seeburg
JENNIFER	Jody Ippolito
LISA	Courtney Ray
MAGGIE	Pebble Kranz

CHARACTERS

Patty . . . . *Juliet*
Chris . . . . *Romeo*
Maggie . . . . *Assistant Director*
Jennifer . . . . *Nurse*
Lisa . . . . *Prompter*

SETTING

The stage is set for a rehearsal of "Act Three, Scene Five" of ROMEO AND JULIET. Juliet's bedroom is established by a rehearsal box. Indeed, all the set pieces can be made of rehearsal boxes, including the balcony, stage right. A bench downstage of the balcony represents the garden. Offstage left is the "rest of the house."

It is after school — say 4:30 — and a rehearsal is in progress. Patty and Jennifer are in rehearsal skirts. The cast has been at work for some weeks, but are not close to performance level.

Patty, a very pretty girl, is obviously the veteran of several productions. She is more confident about her talents than she should be, and her acting is more showy than sensitive. She is not overly tolerant of Chris's more inexperienced approach to theater. Although he is undoubtedly a more natural and probably more talented actor — he is an athlete with an athlete's grace — he is unsure about the theater. This is his first role, and he is frightened by his own shortcomings. He attempts to mask his fear through clowning.

As the scene begins, Patty and Chris are on the platform stage right, the "balcony." Jennifer is a bit off left, waiting her entrance. Lisa is sitting on the floor down center, holding the script of ROMEO AND JULIET. Maggie is observing from the house.

ACT THREE, SCENE FIVE

CHRIS.
Let me be ta'en, let me be put to death;
I am content, so thou wilt have it so.
I'll say yon grey is not the morning's eye,
'Tis but the pale reflex of Cynthia's brow;
Nor that is not the lark, whose notes do beat
The vaulty heaven so high above our heads.
I have more care to stay than will to go.
Come, death, and welcome! Juliet wills it so.
How is 't, my soul? Let's talk; it is not day.
PATTY.
It is, it is: hie hence, be gone, away!
It is the lark that sings so out of tune,
Straining harsh discords and unpleasing sharps.
Some say the lark makes sweet division;
This is not so, for she divideth us:
Some say the lark and loathed toad change eyes.
O, now I would they had changed voices, too!
Since arm from arm that voice doth us affray.
Hunting thee hence with hunt's-up to the day.
O, now be gone; more light and light it grows.
CHRIS.
More light and light; more dark and dark our woes!
JENNIFER. *(Entering Juliet's room from stage left)* Madam!
PATTY. Nurse?
JENNIFER.
Your lady mother is coming to your chamber:
The day is broke; be wary, look about.

5

ACT THREE, SCENE FIVE

(She exits left)

PATTY.
Then, window, let day in, and let life out.

CHRIS.
Farewell, farewell! One kiss, and I'll descend.

(The kiss is not convincing. They are not overly fond of each other it would appear — although CHRIS attempts more ardor than PATTY does — or, at best, they haven't become comfortable with onstage affection as yet. Somewhat chagrined, CHRIS attempts to leave through the "window" and trips up on the bench. He drops character completely with a heartfelt:) Shit!

MAGGIE. Cut!

LISA. That's not in the—

PATTY. How can I say—

JENNIFER. That's awful. Wait until Mr.—

CHRIS. Oh, dear. O, me, O my O my. I said the "S" word!

MAGGIE. I said cut!

PATTY. How can I say, "Art thou gone so?" when he—

CHRIS. How am I supposed to get "gone so" when I have to get over that—

MAGGIE. When I say cut, I mean cut. Cut everything! *(She goes to the stage)*

LISA. *(Holding out the script as proof)* Chris, that is not in the—

MAGGIE. He knows that, Lisa, for godsake!

JENNIFER. Do you want me to get Mr. Wilson?

MAGGIE. I don't want anybody to do anything except shut up for a minute! *(They all do)* We're supposed to be rehearsing the play. You know, the one Shakespeare

ACT THREE, SCENE FIVE

wrote? Shakespeare wrote, "He descends—"

LISA. He goeth down. *(Maggie glares at Lisa, who holds up the script in self-defense)* Right here, "He goeth down."

MAGGIE. *(Barely holds her temper, and then turns to Chris)* Shakespeare wrote, "He goeth down." Shakespeare did not write, "Romeo ad libs all his favorite four letter words as he exits."

CHRIS. Shakespeare did not write, "Romeo has to damn near kill himself every rehearsal by crawling over some stupid bench that falls over all the time while Romeo is trying to spout some stupid iambic pentameter," either.

MAGGIE. Spouting is about right.

CHRIS. Oh?

PATTY. And what is that supposed to mean?

MAGGIE. This is supposed to be a love story. You two are the lovers: Romeo and Juliet. You. You are supposed to care about each other.

PATTY. Mr. Wilson said he liked what we were doing. He said he believed us.

MAGGIE. Don't believe him.

JENNIFER. Don't believe Mr. Wilson?

MAGGIE. I don't believe you.

PATTY. You don't have to.

MAGGIE. The audience won't believe you.

JENNIFER. You're not the director.

MAGGIE. I am the assistant director, and right now I am trying to assist. Mr. Wilson tells you he believes you because he wants you to have confidence. That's fine, but we open in three weeks, and you have to have more than confidence. You have to know what you're doing, what you're saying.

PATTY. And what makes you the expert?

MAGGIE. I listen to you guys. I watch you. Half the time you don't know what you're saying. It's just a bunch of words coming out.

CHRIS. Look, I don't write 'em; I just say 'em.

MAGGIE. How can you say things when you don't know what they mean? When you say, "Jocund day stands tiptoe upon misty mountain top," what are you saying? What do you mean?

CHRIS. It's not supposed to mean anything; it's poetry.

MAGGIE. Poetry always means something.

CHRIS. So?

MAGGIE. So?

CHRIS. So what does it mean, Miss Assistant Director?

MAGGIE. You are Romeo. You have been saying "jocund day" for four weeks now. What do you mean?

CHRIS. You're a real pain, you know?

JENNIFER. I know what jocund means.

MAGGIE. It's not your line.

JENNIFER. But I know what it means.

CHRIS. Super! You play Romeo! Probably good for a few laughs, anyway. The first lesbian production!

JENNIFER. I'm going to tell Mr. Wilson what you— PATTY. That's really disgusting!

MAGGIE. Nice! Real nice, Chris! You probably think jocund is something you wear under your sweatpants.

CHRIS. Just because I spend my time doing other things than always being in—

LISA. Here it is, in a footnote. *(Holding up the script)* Jocund means—

ACT THREE, SCENE FIVE

MAGGIE. Merry.
LISA. Happy.
MAGGIE. Happy.
CHRIS. I'm really "jocund" to know that, Maggie. Really, I am. That will change my whole approach to the line. I'll smile like this. *(He grins broadly)* And twirl my finger in the air like this. *(He does)* "And jocund day stands tiptoe *(He stands on his tiptoes)* upon the misty mountain top."

JENNIFER. *(As she and PATTY can't help laughing)* I don't think Mr. Wilson would like that.

CHRIS. *(Playing his audience)* I'm kind of stuck on "misty mountain top." *(To LISA, who has begun to point out another footnote)* No, don't tell me. Misty, I know. It's how to make the audience *(With emphasis, for MAGGIE)* believe it. Maybe if I just—*(He makes the sound of wind whistling while he swims through the heavy fog of the misty mountain top)*

MAGGIE. *(Not at all pleased by his fooling around, or by the obvious enjoyment of the rest of the cast)* At least you'd be doing something.

PATTY. You know, it's really none of your—

MAGGIE. "Some say the lark and loathed toad change eyes." What do you mean?

PATTY. That means they change. Just like it says. *(Pause)* It means what is says, for godsake! It means they change eyes...some say.

MAGGIE. What did Mr. Wilson say about that line?
PATTY. Louder.
MAGGIE. Louder?
PATTY. Louder.
JENNIFER. *(Ever on PATTY'S side)* He said to say it

louder.

MAGGIE. And that's all?

PATTY. And look out the window.

MAGGIE. And what about Romeo? *(PATTY doesn't understand the question)* While you're looking out the window and being louder, what does Juliet think about him?

CHRIS. Yeh, good question. What about me? What's old Romeo doing all the time the lark and the loathed toad are swapping eyeballs *(He mimes the swap, complete with sound effects)* ...some say.

MAGGIE. *(Pointedly ignoring him)* You are with Romeo. He is your husband. Your *new* husband. He's your lover.

CHRIS. You're a better director than I thought.

PATTY. Maggie, you can just stop this kind of—

MAGGIE. You've just spent your first night alone together.

CHRIS. Talking about larks and loathed toads. I mean, what else is there to talk about, right? *(As if he were beginning a formal lecture.)* Consider the salamander—

MAGGIE. Patty, this is Juliet's bridal night. Morning. This is the first time, ever, that...she...ever...

LISA. *(Who can't stand the silence anymore)* What???

JENNIFER. *(Eyes on heaven)* Oh, my God...

CHRIS. Let's not forget the night on the balcony. I'm not sure Willie told the whole story there. Would a guy like the one you see before you—and I really think Romeo was my kind of guy—crawl all the way up and down the shrubbery for a little kiss? Does that make sense?

ACT THREE, SCENE FIVE

MAGGIE. Chris!

CHRIS. I'm asking you as the assistant director. Nothing personal, believe me. This is a theatrical situation we're discussing here. You helped me out on "jocund" a lot. I really appreciate that. Now this first night business seems even more important than jocund and eyeballs. Am I right?

PATTY. If Mr. Wilson wanted us to think about all this, he'd tell us. I don't know why you think you know better than he does.

JENNIFER. He's been directing for over thirty years.

PATTY. He ought to know what we're supposed to think about. And he doesn't embarrass us by asking us such personal questions.

JENNIFER. Do you think you're smarter than Mr. Wilson?

MAGGIE. If you're acting, you have to be personal. And no, I do not think I am smarter than Mr. Wilson. He can't do everything by himself. He's out picking up props now, and he asked me to run this rehearsal for him. So let's rehearse and learn what it is we're doing. I'm just trying to help you understand Juliet.

PATTY. If you understand Juliet so much better than I do, why didn't Mr. Wilson cast you? You auditioned, just like everybody else. He chose me.

MAGGIE. *(After a moment's hesitation)* He cast you as Juliet because you look like Juliet. You have always looked like Juliet, so you play Juliet. I have always looked like Lady Capulet, so I play Lady Capulet. I play the girlfriends, the mothers, the ladies in the town, the chorus. You play the Juliets.

PATTY. You're not trying to help! You're jealous! You think you know so much, and you're trying to make me out to be some dummy! Well, I'm not! We'll see what Mr. Wilson has to say about your "assisting" when he gets back! If he wants you to play the part, *(She throws her rehearsal skirt at MAGGIE'S feet)* he can have you! *(She rushes out)*

JENNIFER. Patty! Patty! *(To MAGGIE)* Mr. Wilson isn't going to like this. What if she quits! *(She starts to rush out after PATTY, just as PATTY rushes back in)*

PATTY. And I'm not sorry I look like Juliet! That's your problem, not mine! *(She is immediately out again, with JENNIFER in pursuit. We hear JENNIFER'S "Patty, Patty, when did we ever listen to Maggie before..." as they go down the hallway)*

CHRIS. *(After an awkward silence during which LISA picks up PATTY'S rehearsal skirt)* Well, I guess that about wraps it up for today, boys and girls.

MAGGIE. That does not wrap it up. Just because the fair Juliet can't stand a little constructive criticism doesn't mean we quit. We'll rehearse until 5:30, like we're supposed to. *(She looks at LISA, who takes the skirt and goes back to her prompt book)*

CHRIS. Romeo rehearse without Juliet? True, the play is about Romeo, a young man in search of major physical and occasional spiritual fulfillment, an odyssey taking us from callow youth through painful if enlightening experience to a brief but tragic maturity. But still, all-in-all, it is called ROMEO *AND* JULIET. Maybe we should just do ROMEO, the first one-man performance of an age-old classic. At last! The story Shakespeare really

ACT THREE, SCENE FIVE

wished to write, told in some of his own words, unencumbered by superflous characters, uncluttered by meaningless subplots. I say *(He smiles)* jocund, they laugh; I say *(He frowns)* loathed toad, they cry. ROMEO AND JULIET!

MAGGIE. Just because I'm curious, why did you try out?

CHRIS. I thought it would be a kick, parading around in tights and sword fighting. *(He mocks sword fights)* Erroll Flynn lives!

MAGGIE. Is that all?

CHRIS. Having all the girls call me Romeo.

MAGGIE. All?

CHRIS. Present company excepted, of course.

MAGGIE. Thank you.

CHRIS. My pleasure. *(Pause)* So I thought Patty would probably be Juliet. So what? Nothing wrong with that, is there? I figured we'd make an excellent couple.

MAGGIE. You will excuse my pointing out that you've been striking out.

CHRIS. Thank you.

MAGGIE. My pleasure.

CHRIS. *(In frustration)* It's a drag, is what it is—all this rehearsing, learning all these stupid lines.

MAGGIE. Stupid lines? *Romeo And Juliet* is one of the most beautiful dramas ever written.

CHRIS. Yeh, yeh, yeh. "Night's candles are burnt out and jocund day stands tiptoe on the misty mountain top" is stupid. Why doesn't he just say it's morning.

MAGGIE. It's morning.

CHRIS. Yeh—it's morning. Thanks a lot, I really

enjoyed it, but the birds are chirping and I gotta cut out. It's morning.

MAGGIE. So why didn't this stupid playwright just say it's morning?

CHRIS. You're the one who's calling *him* stupid.

MAGGIE. Just borrowing a phrase.

CHRIS. You're the straight-A, honor-roll, National Merit, assistant director. You tell me.

MAGGIE. Don't pull that crap. You're as honor roll as I am. You know, you're probably right. After all these years, someone finally found Shakespeare out. Stupid! Right! We'll do the scene. Your way.

CHRIS. As a monologue?

LISA. I'll read Juliet's lines.

MAGGIE. I'll do Juliet.

LISA. But I've got the script right here.

MAGGIE. *(As if using the script were the stupidest of ideas)* We won't be using the script!

LISA. Then what am I supposed to—

CHRIS. Aren't we versatile! First the assistant director, and now the actress. Juliet, no less.

MAGGIE. If it gets too difficult for you, just close your eyes and think of Patty.

CHRIS. There's a limit to my imagination.

MAGGIE. No kidding! *(They glare at each other)* You're over by the window. *(He goes. MAGGIE parodies PATTY'S Juliet)* Are you going?

CHRIS. Is that all you're going to say?

MAGGIE. That's what Juliet says. It's still night, are you going? And then you say, it's morning. Okay. It's still night, are you going?

ACT THREE, SCENE FIVE 15

CHRIS. It's morning.

MAGGIE. That's not sunlight; it's just a meteor. Stay.

CHRIS. Let me be tak'en—

MAGGIE. No, no, no. No stupid poetry. Just, I'll stay and die. It's just a meteor. Stay.

CHRIS. I'll stay and die.

MAGGIE. No. Go. Then the Nurse comes in.

LISA. Do you want me to—

MAGGIE. No, that's all right.

LISA. *(Under her breath)* I don't see why I don't ever get to—

MAGGIE. She says, "Madam...blah, blah, blah...be wary, look about." Then I say open the window, day's in, you're out. And then you—

CHRIS. *(She is uncomfortable. He loves it)* And then...I kiss you. *(He slowly approaches her. She is flustered and starts to back away)* This is Romeo kissing Juliet, right? I'll never get it right in performance if I don't explore every possibility, every nuance in rehearsal. *(She offers her cheek)* Oh, wow! A cheek! This after our first night together? We must have had a pretty wild time, eh? *(He takes her face in his hands and slowly turns her face to his. He holds it a while, looking into her eyes. Then—just as she is expecting the worst—he smacks her loudly on the nose, laughs, and crosses back to the "balcony," saying ála jive talk)* And then I...goeth down.

MAGGIE. *(Much relieved, laughing)* And you do not say shit.

LISA. *(Shocked)* Maggie!

CHRIS. *(Laughing)* And I do not say shit.

MAGGIE. Really beautiful scene that way. Short. To the point. No stupid poetry. "It's morning." You're out of there.

CHRIS. *(Enjoying her, in spite of himself)* Okay.

MAGGIE. Okay, what?

CHRIS. Okay, you're right. Okay? Okay. That way, it's...nothing.

MAGGIE. Oh? He stays, he gets caught; he gets caught... *(She gestures slitting her throat)* Down the vines, home free.

CHRIS. I don't think he wants to leave.

MAGGIE. You think he wants to stay and get killed?

CHRIS. No, that's stupid.

MAGGIE. That's Shakespeare.

CHRIS. No. I mean it's stupid to stay around. Romeo. But he has to.

MAGGIE. Why?

CHRIS. Because of Juliet.

MAGGIE. Why because of Juliet?

CHRIS. Because he loves her.

MAGGIE. That much?

CHRIS. I guess so.

MAGGIE. That's stupid.

CHRIS. Can we stop using that word?

MAGGIE. Agreed. I didn't mean stupid in terms of... *(She touches her forehead with her finger)* stupid. I mean thoughtless. I mean headstrong. I mean young. I mean fifteen years old.

CHRIS. That's my problem, right there. Romeo is so immature. I'm having trouble remembering that far back.

MAGGIE. *(Ala Viennese)* Try to think back. Remember your first girlfriend.

CHRIS. *(Deep into analysis)* Rhonda Stewart. Blue hair

ACT THREE, SCENE FIVE 17

ribbons. A yellow crayon. *(He draws each figure with his eyes closed)* Sky...house...doggie...everything yellow.

MAGGIE. Perhaps something more recent? *(No response)* Patty? *(She sees she has hurt him)* Sorry.

CHRIS. *(Attempted humour)* Not to worry.

MAGGIE. *(To his rescue)* Remember I told Patty this was Juliet's first night...alone...with a man. Well, it was probably the first night for Romeo...with a woman.

CHRIS. *(Ultra macho)* Listen, you're Lady Capulet, and you aren't around when I talk to Mercutio and Benvolio and the guys about various chicks of Verona.

MAGGIE. Haven't you...I mean, don't you hear that in the locker room all the time? Do you believe everything your friends say about... *(Including LISA)* us?

LISA. Yeh.

CHRIS. His first night. His first...time. You think? *(She nods)* So that's—

MAGGIE. Why—

CHRIS. He doesn't want to go.

MAGGIE. So Shakespeare—

CHRIS. Has them—

MAGGIE. Talk on and on, so—

CHRIS. He won't go. He talks because he doesn't want to go.

MAGGIE. And she talks because she knows he should, but—

CHRIS. She doesn't want him to go. He has to, but he doesn't want to, so he stays and talks and talks—

MAGGIE. And she talks and talks about—

CHRIS. The jocund day—

MAGGIE. And loathed toads—

ACT THREE, SCENE FIVE

MAGGIE and CHRIS. *(Together)* And all that other stupid poetry stuff! *(They dissolve together in laughter)*

CHRIS. That—

MAGGIE. Stupid—

CHRIS. Old—

MAGGIE and CHRIS. *(Together)* Shakespeare! *(Again, gales of shared laughter)*

CHRIS. *(When he can talk)* Thanks.

MAGGIE. It was your idea. You were the one who said he didn't want to go.

CHRIS. But I didn't know why.

MAGGIE. You knew it. *(Pause. Sincerely)* You did.

CHRIS. Can we try the scene again?

MAGGIE. Okay. *(Again, the parody)* It's still night. Are you going? *(They laugh again)*

CHRIS. No. I mean old Willie's way.

MAGGIE. Sounds awfully traditional to me.

CHRIS. I'll try to do better this time, Maggie. Honestly, I will.

MAGGIE. I know.

CHRIS. I'll need help.

MAGGIE. So will I.

CHRIS. No, not you.

MAGGIE. Yes, me. It's one thing to give advice from outfront. I can tell Patty what to do as Juliet. Doing Juliet is something else. She just walks onstage, she's halfway there. Every guy in the audience is already in love with her.

CHRIS. She's not as beautiful as she thinks she is.

MAGGIE. That still leaves room for lots of beauty.

CHRIS. I think she gets less beautiful the longer you're

ACT THREE, SCENE FIVE

around her. I don't mean she's not... *(He tries to mime PAT-TY'S physical attributes, but feels very awkward)*

MAGGIE. Beautiful.

CHRIS. *(Gratefully, he nods assent)* But some girls get more...beautiful...the longer you're... *(He is stuck)*

MAGGIE. Around them. *(He nods assent. They look at each for a moment. Then MAGGIE breaks the clumsy silence)* Let's rehearse. *Romeo And Juliet,* Act Three, Scene Five. *(They get into their places onstage)*

LISA. Do you want me to do your lines this time?

MAGGIE. Thank you, Lisa. I think I know them.

LISA. You're Lady Capulet.

MAGGIE. I knew Juliet's lines before we started. *(To CHRIS)* You never know when they'll come in handy. Shall we? *(CHRIS nods his assent and goes to his place on the stage. They begin the scene. Although she does not have PATTY'S familiarity with the role, it is obvious she has great feeling for the character and the relationship with Romeo. Where PATTY'S acting was more pronounced, MAGGIE'S is more understated, more honest. CHRIS begins to grow in his role as the scene progresses)*

Wilt thou be gone? It is not yet near day:
It was the nightingale, and not the lark,
That pierced the fearful follow of thine ear;
Nightly she sings on yon pomegranate-tree:
Believe me, love, it was the nightingale.

CHRIS.

It was the lark, the hearld of the morn,
No nightingale: look, love, what envious streaks
Do lace the severing clouds in yonder east:
Night's candles are burnt out, and jocund day

Stands tiptoe on the misty mountain tops.
I must be gone and live, or stay and die.
 MAGGIE.
Yon light is not daylight, I know it, I:
It is some meteor that the sun exhales,
To be to thee this night a torch-bearer,
And light thee on thy way to Mantua:
Therefore stay yet: thou need'st not be gone.
 LISA. *(After waiting for CHRIS to come in on cue)* Let me be ta'en—
 CHRIS. I know the line. *(To MAGGIE)* Sorry.
 LISA. That's okay.
 CHRIS. I was listening to you, and I forgot I was supposed to say anything. I never heard it like that before.
 MAGGIE. Thank you.
 CHRIS. I never knew how...afraid Juliet was, that she'd lose something she...cared about...a lot. *(Erupting)* You're why I tried out!
 MAGGIE. What?
 CHRIS. Not Patty. And it wasn't just to strut around in tights, either.
 MAGGIE. Chris, I don't—
 CHRIS. It wasn't that Romeo stuff; I just said that. I saw all three performances of *Our Town* last year. I went the first night because I had to, for English. I was sitting with Rob and we were laughing at Curt becuase he was doing that stupid—sorry—milkman, so he could get out of writing a paper. Then you did that part in the wedding scene where you talked right at the audience about how terrible it is for kids to get married. And the whole

audience got real quiet. And you cried. *(Slight pause)* And I started to cry, and I didn't know why, and Rob was giggling, and I got mad at him, and I left him and sat alone in the balcony for the last act. And then you had that part at the end when Emily comes back and says goodbye to everyone, and I cried again.

MAGGIE. *(Moved)* Chris—

CHRIS. That's the first time I've cried since fourth grade.

MAGGIE. That's sweet.

CHRIS. I hated it! So I went back Friday night, just to show I could do it—sit there without crying.

MAGGIE. And?

CHRIS. Again. Both acts. Both acts, both nights. Saturday, I was three for three. I want to be able to do that.

MAGGIE. Do what?

CHRIS. Make people do that. Laugh when you want them to, cry when you want them to. Make them do whatever you want them to do whenever you want them to. I have people cheering for me at the soccer games sometimes, but it's always a fluke when everything works out right. *(A director should feel free to substitute another sport in this scene, depending upon the actor who plays CHRIS)* Sometimes I dribble pretty well, and sometimes I don't. Sometimes the ball is wet, and I miss it—

MAGGIE. And sometimes the ball is dry and you miss it.

CHRIS. Were you there? Acton?

MAGGIE. *(Smiling)* Yes.

CHRIS. *(Self-mocking)* God, was I awful! Nobody near

me, and I shot right over the post.

MAGGIE. You hardly ever miss.

CHRIS. Sometimes. Sometimes I leave the defensive back eating my dust, and sometimes I don't. The goalie for Ridgely? All-state! I couldn't get it past him the whole game. I mean, here I am, right? *The* center forward! Do I have the crowds cheering for me, waving flags, holding up victory signs when I come out? Sometimes! Larchmont—yes. Three assists and two goals. Ridgely—blanked. But people laughed with you and cried with you and gave you standing ovations every night.

MAGGIE. Chris, they were doing that for the whole cast.

CHRIS. No, they weren't. For you and for Mark, and maybe for Anne, but not for everybody. Patty had all those good lines as Emily, but it was hard to really feel sorry for her or like her a lot. They weren't dumb; they were standing up for you. And they should have. You were in absolute control every second. And the part that got me was I never could figure out how you did it. You were just a mother with a daughter, but every time it was exactly the same. And every time I cried.

MAGGIE. *(Thrilled)* Both acts.

CHRIS. Both acts, three nights. And I wanted to see if I could do that.

MAGGIE. So you tried out for *Romeo And Juliet?*

CHRIS. Yeh. I figured, what could be tougher than soccer?

MAGGIE. And?

CHRIS. This acting stuff is hard.

MAGGIE. It's just being another person. Letting your-

ACT THREE, SCENE FIVE

self be another person.

CHRIS. For you, maybe. *(Confessional)* I know I am going to look stupid. Right up in front of everybody. In tights and all the spotlights on me and five hundred people out there listening to me say, "Night's candles are burnt out, and jocund day stands tiptoe on the misty mountain tops," and Rob and Curt are pointing at me and giggling.

MAGGIE. Rob and Curt graduated.

CHRIS. Robs and Curts never granduate. They go to every play. Everywhere.

MAGGIE. So that's why you clown around in rehearsals so much.

CHRIS. Laugh with them, and you don't get laughed at.

MAGGIE. They don't count.

CHRIS. *(He looks at her. Then)* But you do. I was afraid you would laugh. If you saw me really trying, doing my best, and it was awful—that you'd laugh.

MAGGIE. I wouldn't do that.

CHRIS. No?

MAGGIE. I won't laugh. And nobody else will. Only when you want them to. And they'll cry when you want them to. They'll feel better about themselves because you let them know it's all right to laugh and to cry.

CHRIS. What do I do?

MAGGIE. For openers, don't act at me.

CHRIS. What do you mean?

MAGGIE. Do, "I have more care to stay than will to go."

CHRIS. Now?

ACT THREE, SCENE FIVE

MAGGIE. Now. Just the way you've been rehearsing it.

CHRIS. *(Self-consciously, but accurately reproducing his heavy-handed style)* I have more care to stay than will to go. *(Pause)* Well?

MAGGIE. *(Not unkindly)* It was...loud.

CHRIS. Mr. Wilson always says louder.

MAGGIE and CHRIS. *(Together, enjoying it)* Do it for the deaf old lady in the last row of the balcony!

MAGGIE. Let's forget her for the moment. You're Romeo, I'm Juliet. There's nobody else around.

LISA. Thanks.

MAGGIE. *(Startled. She has forgotten someone else is there)* Lisa!

LISA. Sorry.

MAGGIE. I didn't mean that. *(To CHRIS)* Don't act the line for the balcony. Just talk to me. Romeo is telling Juliet he loves her. That's all. Just the two of them, alone. Just tell me that, that you love me.

CHRIS. *(More simply, more honestly than before.)* I have more care to stay than will to go. *(MAGGIE touches his cheek gently with her hand. It feels right to CHRIS. He continues)* Come, death, and welcome! Juliet wills it so. How is't, my soul? Let's talk; it is not day.

MAGGIE.
It is, it is: hie hence, be gone, away!
It is the lark that sings so out of tune,
Straining harsh discords and unpleasing sharps.
Some say the lark makes sweet division;
This is not so, for she divideth us:
Some say the lark and loathed toad change eyes.

ACT THREE, SCENE FIVE

O, now I would they had changed voices, too!
Since arm from arm that voice doth us affray.
Hunting thee hence with hunt's-up to the day.
O, now be gone; more light and light it grows.

CHRIS. More light and light; more dark and dark our woes.

LISA.
Your lady mother is coming to your chamber;
The day is broke; be wary, look about.

MAGGIE. Then, window, let day in, and let life out.

CHRIS. Farewell, farewell! One kiss, and I'll descend. *(He kisses MAGGIE. It is a good kiss for both of them. They do not rush it. He slowly leaves her and goes to the window. Then he comes back and kisses her again. This is even better)*

LISA. Hey! You're not supposed to do that! *(They are still kissing)* That's not the blocking! *(They finally finish the kiss)* You're not supposed to—

CHRIS. I don't think he could leave with just one kiss like that.

LISA. It says, one kiss. "One kiss, and I'll descend."

CHRIS. *(To MAGGIE)* You're the director.

MAGGIE. I'm the *(He says it with her)* assistant director.

CHRIS. What do you think?

MAGGIE. I like it.

CHRIS. Do you think it works?

MAGGIE. I know it works. What about you?

CHRIS. Oh, I think it works. I do. We probably ought to try it again. Make sure.

LISA. Maggie, Mr. Wilson is not going to like it if you—

CHRIS. *(Ignoring her completely)* Shall we go back to, "One kiss, and I'll descend"?

LISA. *One* kiss!

MAGGIE. I like the way you did. "More light and light." Let's go back to there.

CHRIS. Thanks. Okay, I'm over here. You're there, okay?

MAGGIE. Okay. I'll cue you.

CHRIS. Okay.

MAGGIE. O, now be gone; more light and light it grows.

CHRIS. More light and light; more dark and dark our woes!

MAGGIE. *(After waiting for LISA to do the Nurse)* Lisa!

LISA. *(Not at all happy.)* Madam!

MAGGIE. Nurse?

LISA.
Your lady mother is coming to your chamber;
The day is broke; be wary, look about.

MAGGIE.
Then, window, let day in, and let life out.

CHRIS.
Farewell, farewell! One kiss, and I'll descend.

(He goes to MAGGIE. They are both very ready for the kiss, but just as he reaches her, PATTY and JENNIFER burst in)

PATTY. Mr. Wilson is back. He'll be here in a few minutes.

JENNIFER. He's not very happy with you, Maggie— about your directing, and getting Patty upset like that.

LISA. She's changed his blocking.

JENNIFER. He said to run it one more time, and then

ACT THREE, SCENE FIVE 27

he'll come and see what you've done.

PATTY. What do you mean, she's changed his blocking?

LISA. When he starts to go down—

CHRIS. Goeth down.

LISA. When he starts to leave—

PATTY. Just stick with the original blocking, okay? I have enough trouble with this scene as it is. *(To MAGGIE)* and no more assisting, please!

MAGGIE. I won't say a word. *(To CHRIS, gesturing)* Okay?

CHRIS. *(Smiling, repeating the gesture)* Okay.

MAGGIE. Places, please. Act three, scene five. *(CHRIS and PATTY get into their places onstage. JENNIFER goes off left)*

PATTY. *(She begins coldly, mechanically)*
Wilt thou be gone? It is not yet near day:
It was the nightingale, and not the lark,
That pierced the fearful hollow of thine ear;
Nightly she sings on yon pomergranate-tree:
Believe me, love, it was the nightingale.

CHRIS. *(He is so much improved that, after only a few lines, JENNIFER and PATTY exchange glances and begin to whisper to each other. When CHRIS notices this, he stops his Romeo and says, "What's wrong?")*
It was the lark, the herald of the morn,
No nightingale: look, love, what envious streaks
Do lace the severing clouds in yonder east:
Night's candles are burnt out, and jocund day
Stands tiptoe on the—what's wrong?

ACT THREE, SCENE FIVE

JENNIFER. That's really great, Chris. What an improvement. Mr. Wilson is going to love it.

PATTY. I can't believe it. You're really good. I'm impressed. Let's do it!

CHRIS. *(He looks at MAGGIE, again seated in the house, as he shrugs and smiles. Then he continues his much improved Romeo. PATTY joins him in giving her best Juliet so far. By the time they reach the kiss, the scene is going extremely well)*
It was the lark, the herald of the morn,
No nightingale: look, love, what envious streaks
Do lace the severing clouds in yonder east:
Night's candles are burnt out, and jocund day
Stands tiptoe on the misty mountain tops.
I must be gone and live, or stay and die.

PATTY.
Yon light is not daylight, I know it, I:
It is some meteor that the sun exhales,
To be to thee this night a torch-bearer,
And light thee on thy way to Mantua:
Therefore stay yet: thou need'st not be gone.

CHRIS.
Let me be ta'en, let me be put to death;
I am content, so thou wilt have it so.
I'll say yon grey is not the morning's eye,
'Tis but the pale reflex of Cynthia's brow;
Nor that is not the lark, whose notes do beat
The vaulty heaven so high above our heads.
I have more care to stay than will to go.
Come, death, and welcome! Juliet wills it so.
How is't, my soul? Let's talk; it is not day.

PATTY.
It is, it is: hie hence, be gone, away!

ACT THREE, SCENE FIVE

It is the lark that sings so out of tune,
Straining harsh discords and unpleasing sharps.
Some say the lark makes sweet division;
This is not so, for she divideth us:
Some say the lark and loathed toad change eyes.
O, now I would they had changed voices, too!
Since arm from arm that voice doth us affray.
Hunting thee hence with hunt's-up to the day.
O, now be gone; more light and light it grows.
  CHRIS.
More light and light; more dark and dark our woes!
  JENNIFER. Madam!
  PATTY. Nurse?
  JENNIFER.
Your lady mother is coming to your chamber;
The day is broke; be wary, look about.
  PATTY.
Then, window, let day in, and let life out.
  CHRIS. Farewell, farewell! One kiss, and I'll descend. *(They kiss, and it is a good one. PATTY begins to respond enthusiastically. The kiss continues. LISA says, "Wow." And then after a moment or two she turns to MAGGIE and says, "Maggie, that's good!" JENNIFER, not pleased that PATTY has lost her perspective, warns her quietly, "Patty." Then, with more insistence, "Patty!" MAGGIE watches with mixed emotions. Finally, the kiss ends and CHRIS goes to the balcony. He pauses, then begins to cross back to PATTY. Just before he reaches her, he stops, faces MAGGIE, says)* Patty thinks we ought to stick with the original blocking. What do you think?
  MAGGIE. Good idea. I agree with Patty. If Mr. Wilson wants to change something, he'll change it. One is

definitely enough.

PATTY. What change? One what?

MAGGIE. You're right. I didn't mean to break your concentration. Really, I'm sorry.

PATTY. That's all right.

MAGGIE. Since we're stopped, can I say just one thing?

PATTY. *(Not ready for criticism at all)* What is it?

MAGGIE. That was good. Really good. A nice scene.

PATTY. *(Surprised)* You liked it?

MAGGIE. It liked it. You and Chris work really well together. It's going to be fine.

PATTY. *(Pleased)* You think so?

MAGGIE. I know so.

PATTY. There's still a lot of room for improvement.

MAGGIE. That's why we rehearse.

PATTY. *(Hungry for praise)* Could you hear me all right on "More light and light it grows"?

MAGGIE. I heard you fine. It was nice.

LISA. Me, too. It was.

PATTY. Did you believe it?

MAGGIE. I believed it. I did. The scene got better and better as it went on.

CHRIS. *(Smiling)* Did you believe the kiss? *(No response from MAGGIE)* You know, the one there at the end?

MAGGIE. I know which one.

CHRIS. Did you believe it?

MAGGIE. It looked...okay.

CHRIS. Do you think it was rushed?

MAGGIE. It looked fine from here.

CHRIS. It felt a little rushed. What do you think, Patty?

ACT THREE, SCENE FIVE

PATTY. It might have been a little—
MAGGIE. It was not rushed.
CHRIS. This was their first night together.
MAGGIE. I know.
CHRIS. But you believed it?
MAGGIE. Yes. Yes, I did.
PATTY. Thank you. And you, too, Chris. You did fine, too.
CHRIS. Gee, thanks, Patty.
PATTY. I mean it. Really. It wasn't just me.
CHRIS. *(Oh, so humble)* Ohhh.
MAGGIE. No, she's right, Chris. It wasn't just Patty. It takes two to make a love scene.
MAGGIE and CHRIS. *(Together. Enjoying this)* Romeo *and* Juliet! *(They laugh. Patty joins in, although she is not sure why)*
MAGGIE. Let's just do the ending before Mr. Wilson gets here. So you'll be ready.
JENNIFER. He's going to love this. This is going to be the best.
PATTY. Where from? How about, *(Flirtatiously)* "One kiss, and I'll descend"?
MAGGIE. What do you think, Romeo?
CHRIS. He's probably on his way. We better skip to the end, after, "He goeth down."
MAGGIE. *(Pleased)* Okay, Patty?
PATTY. *(Disappointed)* All right.
CHRIS. I'm here. I have goneth.
MAGGIE. *(To Patty)* You're at the window?
PATTY. Yes. *(She goes to the window and looks "down" at Romeo)*

Art thou gone so? Love, lord, ay, husband, friend!
I must hear from thee every day in the hour,
For, in a minute there are many days:
O, by this count I shall be much in years
Ere I again behold my Romeo!

CHRIS. *(Facing Patty)* Farewell! *(During this line, he turns and faces Maggie directly and says to her)* I will omit no opportunity that may convey my greetings, love, to thee.

PATTY. Aren't you supposed to be facing me on that line? Is that where you changed the blockings?

CHRIS. Mr. Wilson always tells me to cheat out, not to face upstage because the audience can't hear me. They can't see my face.

PATTY. Well, now I can't see you. You're supposed to be saying goodbye to me, and I can't see you.

CHRIS. What do you think, assistant director? Should I do *(As he faces Patty and says just a bit mechanically)* "I will omit no opportunity that may convey my greetings, love, to thee"? or *(As he faces Maggie directly and says with more feeling)* "I will omit no opportunity that may convey my greetings, love, to thee"? Well, what do you think?

JENNIFER. I like it both ways.

LISA. Me, too.

CHRIS. *(To Maggie)* What do you think?

PATTY. I couldn't see him the second time.

CHRIS. Well?

MAGGIE. I think we better leave that up to Mr. Wilson. Jen, why don't you tell him we're ready to run the scene, okay?

JENNIFER. I'll get him. *(As she leaves)* He's going to love it.

ACT THREE, SCENE FIVE 33

PATTY. It really feels so much better, Maggie. Thanks for helping Chris. Oh, and me, too.

CHRIS. Yes, thanks, Maggie. I really appreciate it. I need some help on the balcony scene. Do you think we could work on that over the weekend? I'm having a lot of trouble with, "It is my lady, O, it is my love! O, that she knew she were!"

PATTY. *(At her most seductive)* I can help you with that. You could come over, and I could help you work out the kinks.

CHRIS. *(Goes to Patty)* Gee, thanks, Patty. That's great. But you're so far ahead of me already *(Goes to Maggie)*, I think it might be better for me to work with Maggie. I hate to waste your time until I catch up a little. Not that I ever will, but I know I slow you down.

PATTY. But you're getting a lot better. You really are starting to get a grasp on your character.

CHRIS. That's great. Thanks, that really is. Maybe one weekend with Maggie on the balcony scene, and I'll be there. What do you say, Maggie?

MAGGIE. I'll be at my window Saturday night.

CHRIS. I'll bring the ladder.

MAGGIE. My dad has one in the garage. Says any boy wants to use it, it's okay.

CHRIS. Nice guy.

MAGGIE. A prince.

CHRIS. Eight o'clock.

But soft! What light through yonder window breaks?
It is the east, and *(To Maggie)* Juliet is the sun.
Arise fair sun, and kill the *(To Patty)* envious moon,
Who is already sick and pale with grief,

That *(Maggie)* thou her maid art far more fair *(Patty)* than she.

MAGGIE. We'll work on it.

CHRIS. Thanks, coach. Do you think if I improve, I can get you to believe it?

MAGGIE. Yes.

PATTY. I believe it already.

LISA. Me, too.

CHRIS. *(All he has heard is Maggie's, "Yes")* Can't ask for more than that.

JENNIFER. *(Rushing in)* He's coming.

MAGGIE. Places, everybody.

JENNIFER. I told him how good it was. He's really excited.

MAGGIE. ROMEO AND JULIET. Act Three, Scene Five. *(CHRIS and PATTY are in place, ready for "Wilt thou be gone?")*

THE END

OTHER TITLES AVAILABLE FROM BAKERS PLAYS

IN JULIET'S GARDEN

Judy Elliot McDonald

Competition, College, High School / Comedy / 7 women (1 man optional) / Simple unit set

Juliet Capulet invites four other heroines of Shakespeare's classics (Katharina, Portia, Ophelia and Desdemona) to lunch in her favorite garden in Verona to discuss 'issues' they all have with their plots. All the ladies have suggestions how these issues might be remedied. Shakespeare has also been invited, but instead sends an envoy, his literary agent and editor Jacqueline de Boys, who attempts to save the day with the help of Juliet's Nurse. This lively fifty-minute one-act comedy sparkles with wit and an in-depth understanding of the characters of these indelible ladies, and their effects on playgoers over the centuries. (Cameo appearance by Shakespeare at the end is optional).

www.ingramcontent.com/pod-product-compliance
Lightning Source LLC
Chambersburg PA
CBHW072339300426
44109CB00042B/1959